ARAL SEA
SPIAN SEA
BACTRIA
R. Murghab
HINDU KUSH
KHYBER PASS
PARTHIA
AFGHANISTAN
DRANGIANA
R. Jhelu
Persepolis
INDIA
R. Indus
CARMANIA
ERSIAN GULF
Patala
Karachi
ARABIAN SEA

Series 561

Alexander the Great, who lived more than two thousand years ago, was not only a great soldier who conquered the whole of the then known world, he was also a wise and just ruler.

This is his story.

A LADYBIRD
HISTORY
BOOK

2/6
NET

AN ADVENTURE FROM HISTORY

ALEXANDER THE GREAT

by

L. DU GARDE PEACH

with illustrations by

JOHN KENNEY

Publishers: Wills & Hepworth Ltd., Loughborough

First published 1963 ©   *Printed in England*

ALEXANDER THE GREAT

Alexander of Macedon was born in the year 356 B.C., more than two thousand years ago. He is known as Alexander the Great because he was one of the greatest soldiers the world has known, as well as a wise and just ruler of men.

When he was a boy his father, King Philip of Macedon, summoned the famous Greek philosopher Aristotle to be his tutor, and it was his teaching which influenced Alexander all his life.

In those days the country we now know as Greece was divided into a number of small kingdoms, and Alexander's father, King Philip, realised that if these kingdoms were joined together, they would be strong enough to resist the Persians who threatened them from the east. Some of the Greek states agreed with Philip, but others resisted, and in the interests of all, Philip was obliged to send expeditions against them.

On one of these expeditions Alexander, at the age of eighteen, was put in command of the left wing of the army. In a battle which broke the power of Thebes, another Greek state, Alexander distinguished himself by his personal courage and wise leadership.

7214 0175 9

When Alexander was twenty years old, his father, King Philip, was assassinated. The Greek states, which Philip had combined in the League of Corinth, immediately tried to break away, believing that the young King would be too weak to prevent them. They were wrong.

With the support of his father's general Antipater, Alexander was crowned King of Macedon, and at once set himself to the task of regaining the leadership of the Greek states. He marched south, and the sight of the Macedonian army caused the Greeks to elect him leader of the League of Corinth in place of his father.

Meanwhile the tribes north of Macedonia, in what is now Bulgaria, threatened his northern borders. In a swift campaign Alexander marched as far as the Danube, overcoming the tribe of the Triballi. But the tribesmen had sent their women and children across the river, and those who escaped from the battle now joined them. Helped by other tribes, they defied Alexander from the further bank.

Ordering his men to cut down trees and make log rafts, Alexander managed to get more than 5,000 men across the Danube. With these he easily dispersed the remaining tribesmen.

A rumour that Alexander had been killed on the Danube caused the Greek states once more to rebel.

Alexander did not hesitate. Gathering his army, he again marched south, learning on the way that the King of Persia was supplying the Greek states with arms and money. In fourteen days he reached the town of Thebes, where the rebellion against him had first broken out.

The Greek states, amongst them Athens and Sparta, waited to see what would happen. Alexander had expected Thebes to surrender, but he was prepared to attack the town if it did not. The Thebans refused, and marching out to meet Alexander's army, were decisively beaten. The Macedonian soldiers entered the town with the fugitives.

Alexander was usually merciful to those whom he had conquered, and would have spared the town and its inhabitants. The other members of the League of Corinth, who were jealous of Thebes, thought differently, and persuaded Alexander to make an example of the rebels. Thebes was completely destroyed, only the temples and the house in which the famous Greek poet Pindar had lived a hundred years before, were spared. Some of the Thebans escaped to Athens, but eight thousand were sold as slaves.

Alexander was now undisputed leader of the Greek states, and he decided to carry out his father's plan: the invasion of Persia.

He had two reasons for doing this. The King of Persia, by name Darius, had helped the Greek states against him, and Alexander knew that Darius was only waiting for an opportunity openly to attack him. The other reason went back a century and a half. In the year 480 B.C., a King of Persia named Xerxes had invaded Macedonia and Greece, and burnt the town of Athens.

Ever since then the Greeks had planned revenge, and now Alexander was able to command a great army of Greeks and Macedonians. With 35,000 men, armed with javelins, bows, and spears fourteen feet long, he crossed the Dardenelles with flags flying from the masts of his gaily painted ships.

The Persian plan was to retreat before Alexander, destroying everything that could be of use to him, until Darius could gather an army strong enough to fight him. As the Persians retreated, Alexander easily beat the small forces which he encountered, and the town of Hallicarnassus, now named Budrum, was successfully besieged. This gave Alexander command of the coast of Asia opposite Greece.

From the coast Alexander turned northwards, fighting his way through the tribes of what is now Turkey, to a town called Gordium. It was here that he did something which is still so well remembered that it has become a figure of speech.

According to the legend, the Greek god Zeus had declared that the first man who drove up to his temple in a wagon should be made king. When one day a peasant called Gordius happened to do this, he was crowned by his countrymen, and founded the town of Gordium.

The story goes on to say that Gordius had fastened the yoke to the pole of the wagon with a very complicated knot, and an oracle had declared that whosoever afterwards should untie the knot, would reign over all Asia.

When Alexander captured the town he was shown the wagon, which had been preserved in the temple. Alexander had every intention of becoming the ruler of all Asia, but he did not waste time trying to untie the knot. Drawing his sword, he cut through it with one stroke. That is why, when anyone solves a difficult problem, we say that they have cut the Gordian knot.

Alexander's intention was not to waste his strength fighting small tribes, but to meet and destroy the Persian army commanded by Darius. He turned south again to Tarsus, and it was here that an incident occurred which gives us an insight into Alexander's character.

He was taken ill with a fever, and just as his doctor, Philippus, was handing him a glass of medicine, he received a letter telling him that Philippus had been bribed by Darius to poison him. Alexander trusted Philippus and, to show his trust, he handed him the letter to read as he drank the medicine.

Darius was equally anxious to destroy the forces of Alexander, and the two armies met at a place called Issus, which was near the coast where Turkey joins up with Syria to-day. Alexander won the battle and founded a city named Alexandria, later called Alexandretta. To-day it is known by the Turkish name, Iskenderun.

Darius fled away eastwards when he saw that the battle was going against him, and after the battle Alexander learned that Darius' mother, wife, and daughters had been captured. He ordered that they should be treated with the greatest respect and supplied with every comfort.

The Persian army had been scattered, but Darius still had a fleet in the Mediterranean. Alexander had not enough ships to fight it at sea, so he decided to capture all the ports at which it obtained supplies. This would make the fleet powerless to do him harm.

All the coast towns of Palestine surrendered to him until he came to Tyre. This city had held out for thirteen years when besieged in a previous war, and its citizens thought that they could safely defy Alexander.

The city of Tyre was built on an island half a mile from the shore, so Alexander ordered a causeway to be built along which his soldiers could attack. Where the water was shallow this was comparatively easy, but near the walls of Tyre it was much deeper, and not only was the work more difficult, but the defenders were able to destroy during the night, the work which had been done during the day.

Alexander's engineers built floating rafts for the heavy catapults, and under cover of their fire the causeway was completed. After a siege of seven months the city was captured by assault. The Persian fleet never troubled Alexander again.

After the capture of Tyre, Alexander continued his march along the coast of the Mediterranean to Egypt. At the delta of the Nile he paused.

Alexander was more than merely a successful general. On all his campaigns he took with him men skilled in science, the arts, and in trade, and he was always ready to listen to what they had to tell him. He knew that every country he conquered meant more trade for the merchants.

Where the Nile enters the sea it is divided into a number of smaller rivers, and here Alexander decided to build a great seaport to which ships could come for all the rich products of Egypt. When later Alexander marched away to lead his armies thousands of miles to the far east, he left behind him architects, engineers, and builders to carry on the work. He never returned to see the city of which he had dreamed.

To this day Alexandria remains a permanent memorial to the great conqueror who caused it to be built. During the centuries since it was founded it has become more and more important, with harbours to which come ships from all over a world which Alexander never knew.

The Egyptians offered no resistance to Alexander. They hailed him as their deliverer from the Persians, and at Memphis crowned him as Pharoah of all Egypt.

In those days men were in the habit of consulting oracles for advice on important undertakings. These were places where the gods were supposed to answer questions put to them by the priests, and the most famous of them was at Delphos, in Greece. Another was the oracle of Ammon, an Egyptian god, at a place three hundred miles across the desert from Alexandria.

It was to this place, now called the Siwa oasis, that Alexander decided to go, in order to ask the oracle whether his campaign against Darius would be successful. There were of course no roads across the desert, and the man who was guiding Alexander lost his way. It was only by following snakes and birds, returning to the oasis, that Alexander finally reached and consulted the oracle.

The priests greeted Alexander as the son of Ammon, because the Pharoah of Egypt was always supposed to be descended from the gods. Whether Alexander believed this or not we do not know. It is possible that he did.

Darius had had a breathing space in which to assemble another army. In order to make it more effective against the foot soldiers, Darius had a number of scythed chariots constructed. These were chariots with long sharp blades attached to the wheels, and when driven at full gallop through a body of men on foot, they inflicted terrible wounds.

Alexander returned from Egypt by way of Damascus, where he captured a vast amount of treasure belonging to Darius. He crossed the two great rivers, the Euphrates and the Tigris, unopposed. On the further side of the Tigris, Darius was waiting for him.

It was on an October morning, in the year 331 B.C., that the two armies came face to face. Alexander had seen to it that his men had a good meal and a night's sleep. The Persians had stood to arms all night, and were weary and hungry.

The battle started and the scythed chariots charged. But Alexander's javelin men opened their ranks and let them through, striking down the horses as they passed. Alexander immediately attacked with his horsemen, and the Persian foot soldiers broke and fled. The way was open for Alexander to enter Babylon in triumph.

Darius had, as usual, fled from the battle, leaving his soldiers to fight or die. Alexander did not immediately pursue him.

At Babylon, Alexander showed himself to be a wise conqueror. He restored all the native customs, and appointed a Persian noble to be the civil governor of the city. Soon his army was again on the march south-eastwards to Persepolis, a hundred miles east of the head of the Persian Gulf.

Alexander forced his soldiers to cover long distances, sometimes as much as thirty-six miles in a day. There was good reason for this. At Persepolis there was more treasure belonging to Darius, and Alexander wanted to get there before it was removed. He succeeded and captured gold said to have been worth forty-four million pounds.

Meanwhile Darius had hurried due east to a place named Ecbatana, which is the modern town of Hamadan. Having captured the treasure, Alexander decided to follow him, but on arriving at Ecbatana he learned that Darius had again left. By forced marches, and finally almost alone, riding fifty miles in a night, Alexander overtook Darius, only to find that he had been killed by two of his own officers.

In Ecbatana Alexander found a wonderful gold and silver palace, and as he sat in the midst of the scented luxury of the East, he realised that at last he was its master.

Aristotle, his old teacher, had taught him that it was as difficult to organise peace as to make war. Alexander was King of Macedonia, but by conquest he was now also King of Persia. His aim was to combine the two kingdoms and the two peoples, the Greeks and the Persians, into one.

To begin with, he appointed Persian nobles, as well as his Greek or Macedonian generals, to be governors of towns and provinces. His second step was to make Babylon the capital of the new empire, an empire which stretched from the Mediterranean to the Caspian sea, and was soon to stretch much further.

This did not please his Greek and Macedonian followers, and they were even less pleased when Alexander changed from his Greek tunic to the flowing robes of the Persians. He adopted a new title, Lord of Asia, and minted coins, which may be seen in museums to-day, bearing the royal lion-gryphon of Persia. He was now only twenty-seven years old.

Alexander was now ready to march eastwards. How far the Persian empire extended he did not know, but he was determined to conquer the whole of it.

He had reached the river Murghab when he learned that the tribes to the south, in what is now Afghanistan, had risen in arms against him. Alexander knew that it would be folly to march eastwards leaving hostile tribes behind him, able to stop his supplies and reinforcements. In a quick campaign he pacified the country and was able to resume his march.

The country in which the army now found itself was without towns or cities. There were only small villages and the palaces of the rulers. Alexander realised that towns were necessary if trade was to be encouraged, so he gave orders for towns to be built. Each was named Alexandria, followed by the name of the province.

The campaign in Afghanistan had meant a big detour to the south. Alexander was now obliged to turn north-eastwards over the snow-covered mountains of the Hindu Kush. The army suffered from lack of food and fuel, and it is recorded that they lived on the flesh of the mules which died.

There were still battles to be fought. A powerful prince named Oxyartes commanded an army holding the mountains to the north. His main stronghold was on a great rock, and the garrison mocked at Alexander, telling him that he would never capture it unless his men could fly.

By driving iron pegs into the cracks of the rocks and using rope ladders, the attacking soldiers managed to reach the top. The defenders were so surprised to see them that they surrendered.

Oxyartes escaped, but amongst those captured was his daughter Roxana. When she was brought before Alexander he saw that she was very beautiful, and within a short time they were married with all the colour and ceremony of a Persian wedding.

This had the desired effect on Oxyartes. When he found that Alexander was ready to form such an alliance with him, he sent messengers asking for peace. There was nothing which Alexander wanted more, and from then onwards Oxyartes was his faithful ally. In this Alexander showed his wisdom. He remembered the teaching of his great master Aristotle, that it is always necessary to make peace after making war. The alliance with Oxyartes secured peace.

Alexander was now in the far north of Afghanistan. It is a country of wild mountains, and to the east there were many tribes which were still hostile.

Strong reinforcements had arrived and he now had an army of 30,000 men ready to advance. They were marching into the unknown, because no-one could tell what was beyond the mountains. Alexander believed that by marching eastwards he would soon come to the sea. If we look at a map we shall see how wrong he was. To reach the sea to the east his army would have had to march right across China.

Alexander first turned south-eastward, in order to cross the mountains by the Khyber pass, a name well known to British soldiers two thousand years later.

After much fighting Alexander reached the river Indus. Beyond it lay the rich country of the Punjab and of a powerful prince named Porus, who commanded a large army with two hundred elephants. By making a wide detour Alexander crossed the river and successfully attacked from behind. When Porus was brought before him, Alexander asked him how he expected to be treated. "Like a king," replied Porus. By this reply he gained Alexander's respect and friendship.

Now that Porus had become his friend, Alexander added hundreds of elephants to his army. These were very valuable because on the march they could carry a great deal of the baggage. In battle horses would not face them, and foot soldiers were almost powerless against them.

After the battle in which Porus was defeated, Alexander founded two cities, both named Alexandria: the first, Alexandria Nicaea, where his army had been encamped, and the second, Alexandria Bucephala.

There is a story connected with the second city which shows us a different side of the nature of the great conqueror. He always rode at the head of his soldiers, and often charged with them in battle. He had of course hundreds of horses, but one of them, named Bucephalus, was his favourite.

Bucephalus had carried Alexander many hundreds of miles across Asia, all the way from Macedonia. Now the horse had died, and Alexander grieved for him as for a friend. To the memory of this, one of the most famous horses in history, he founded a city on the spot where the horse had died. He also had a special coin struck, showing himself on Bucephalus pursuing one of Porus' elephants.

The march continued, always eastwards, with Alexander still expecting and hoping to see the sea from the next hilltop.

Alexander's hopes were not shared by his soldiers. They were now just north of where you will find Amritsar on the map to-day, thousands of miles from their homes in Greece. It was more than eight years since they had crossed the Dardanelles into Asia.

The fighting in the Punjab had been heavy, and many men had been killed and wounded. Those who were left were beginning to wonder how many of them would ever see their homes again. More and more enemies were waiting for them to the east, and they had heard that across the next river there was a tribe which had thousands of very large and fierce elephants.

The army mutinied. The soldiers who had followed Alexander so faithfully and fought so bravely, refused to go any further. This was a great blow to Alexander. He retired to his tent for three days, hoping that the soldiers would change their minds. When they did not, he promised them that they should march for home then and there. The soldiers rejoiced, not knowing that the worst was yet to come.

At first the return journey was easy. Alexander decided to follow the river Jhelum to the sea, and he built or commandeered nearly a thousand ships. Many of the soldiers sailed in the ships; the others marched along the banks of the river with the horses and elephants.

Soon the Jhelum was joined by another river, and here the soldiers quickly found that they had not finished fighting. The campaign was short, but the fighting was hard. One town after another had to be taken by assault, and twice Alexander was obliged to scale the wall first, to encourage his weary and disheartened soldiers to follow him.

On the second occasion even his best soldiers hung back. So Alexander seized a ladder and mounted the wall, followed only by his shield bearer and one of his officers named Leonnatus. Alexander jumped down from the wall into the town and fought single-handed until the other two joined him.

In doing so he was wounded, and Peucestas held his shield over him whilst Leonnatus fought off the enemy. At last, and only just in time, the army broke into the town, and Alexander was carried fainting to one of the ships.

Through all his long marches of thousands of miles across Asia, Alexander had always remembered the teaching of Aristotle. Battles could win an empire, but only trade could hold it together.

So wherever he went, he met and talked with the merchants and traders, always eager to know what they had to sell in the noisy, colourful markets of the east. The old trade routes—later to be travelled by Marco Polo—and the canals which joined one river to another, were all carefully recorded.

Alexander wished to see the whole of the known world open to all merchants, with every kind of merchandise moving freely between east and west. He intended his new cities to be great markets to which traders would bring their goods from all over the world.

To make it easier for the peoples of different countries to trade together, Alexander issued money which was to be used everywhere. The only place which was still to be allowed to mint its own money was Babylon. Unfortunately, when Alexander died, each country went back to its own coinage. Trade between countries would be much simpler to-day if we used the same money all over the world.

Alexander sailed down the river to a place named Patala, not far from the sea. Here he began to build a great harbour to which ships could come from other countries to supply the markets. He was still dreaming of founding a great trading empire.

Already one of his generals had started to march westwards towards home. He took with him the heavy baggage and all the sick and wounded soldiers, as well as all the elephants. He was to join up with the main army later.

Alexander had now reached what to-day we call the Arabian Sea, near Karachi. It was a wonderful moment when first he and his soldiers looked out over what was an ocean unknown to them. Alexander had not reached the sea to the east, but he had found a new ocean to the south.

According to the ancient religion of the Greeks, this was a time for sacrifices to the gods. Alexander poured wine into the water, and then flung the golden goblet far out over the waves, praying that the gods of the seas and winds would bring his ships safely home to port. The ships then sailed away.

About three thousand men sailed up towards the Persian Gulf in the ships. With the rest of the army Alexander now began one of the most terrible marches in history.

His intention was to keep close to the coast, in touch with the ships. As these were not large enough to carry food and water for so many men, they were to be supplied from time to time by the army.

For a hundred miles or so all went well, then Alexander suddenly found that his way along the coast was barred by a range of mountains. He was obliged to march far inland, and as it was wild, unknown country, he took with him some of the natives as guides. Unfortunately when they got away from the coast, they knew no more about the country than he did.

The army became completely lost in wild desert country, without water or food. It was so hot in the daytime that they could march only by night. For two hundred miles they struggled along, eating the baggage animals and burning the wagons for firewood. Those who fell sick had to be left behind, and many hundreds died on the way.

At last they again reached the coast. Alexander was able to rest his men, but there was no sign of the ships. They had sailed on, and it was not until the army had marched another four hundred miles across country that they again came together.

The sailors had met with many adventures. One of these was an encounter with a school of whales. They had never before seen whales, and they thought that they were hostile ships. So they sailed towards them ready for battle, with all their trumpets blowing. They were very surprised when the supposed enemy ships suddenly dived and disappeared.

Again the fleet and the army separated. The ships sailed on up the Persian Gulf, and the army marched by way of Persepolis, which they had occupied years before on their outward march.

At a place which you will find on the map as Ahwaz, near the head of the Persian Gulf, they met again, and a great feast was held. At this feast Alexander ordered eighty of his generals and ten thousand of his men to marry Persian women, to unite the two peoples.

This had been Alexander's great ambition, to unite all the different races of his new great empire into one people. As he had now conquered the whole of the known world, this meant that he was trying to create a world state, in place of a number of countries, small and large, all competing and fighting with one another.

This was a great design, but unfortunately Alexander did not succeed in achieving it. One of the ways in which he tried to do so made his Greek soldiers very angry. They objected when some of his Greek regiments were disbanded and Persians enlisted in place of them. Alexander faced another mutiny.

He gathered the discontented soldiers together and told those who so wished, to go home. "Go, every one of you," he said, "and tell them at home that you deserted your King who had led you from victory to victory across the world."

The mutinous soldiers repented, and again a great feast was held to celebrate the conclusion of peace. Nine thousand guests were at the banquet, and Greeks, Macedonians, and Persians sat together at the King's table. They poured out offerings of wine to the gods as the trumpets sounded.

At this banquet Alexander made a great speech in which he prayed that all the peoples of the world might live together happily and peacefully. Since then, for two thousand years, statesmen have been trying unsuccessfully to bring this about.

Whether Alexander would have succeeded we do not know. He did not live long enough to make the attempt, for he was dead within a year.

It was at Babylon that Alexander prepared for another great expedition, this time a peaceful one. He caused a great harbour to be excavated and a thousand ships to be built. With these he meant to explore all the coastline round Arabia, to try to find a sea route from Babylon to Egypt.

Three days before the date fixed for the sailing of the fleet, Alexander was taken ill. It is possible that he was poisoned. There were many Persians in his camp who pretended to be friendly, but who hated him for having conquered their country. Although he grew rapidly weaker, he continued to direct the preparations for the expedition. It was too late. At the age of thirty-two he died, far from his homeland, King of an empire he was never to rule.

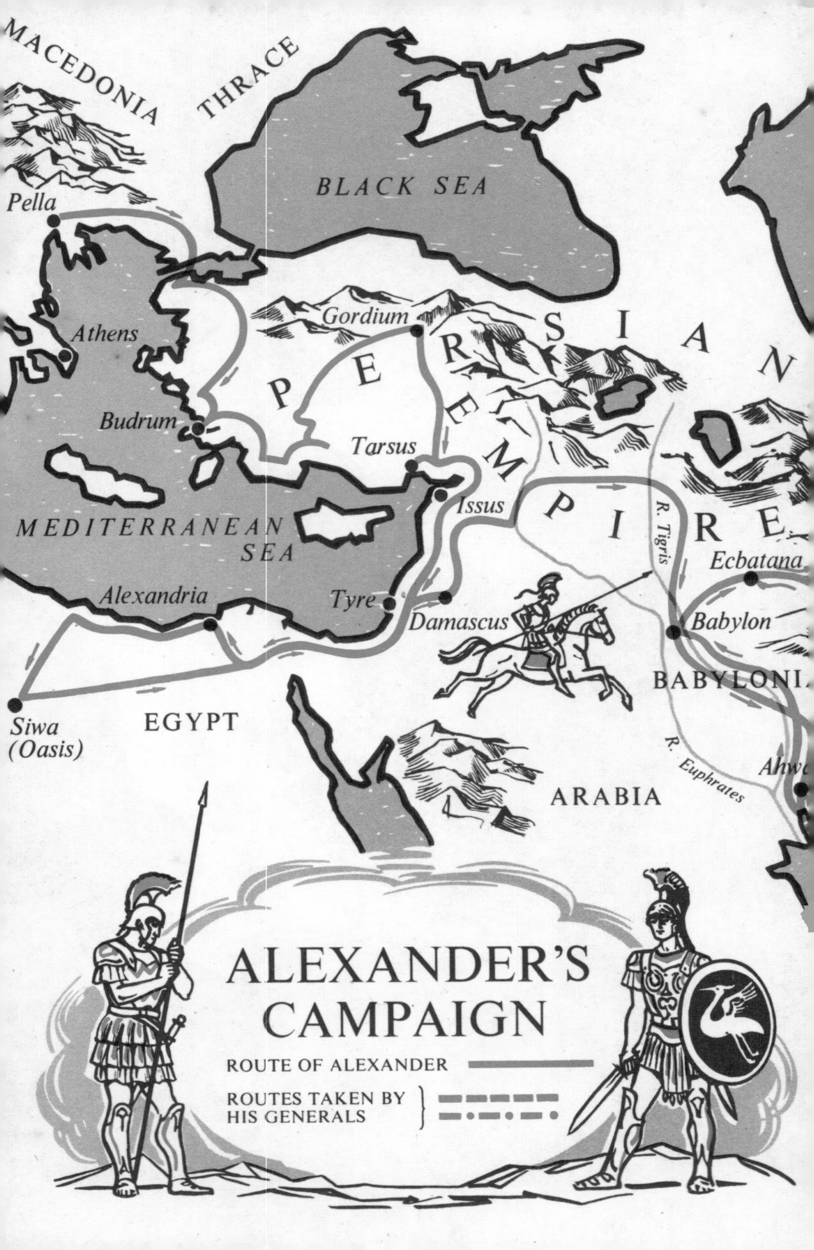

MACEDONIA
THRACE
BLACK SEA
Pella
Athens
Gordium
PERSIAN EMPIRE
Budrum
Tarsus
Issus
MEDITERRANEAN SEA
R. Tigris
Ecbatana
Alexandria
Tyre
Damascus
Babylon
BABYLONI
Siwa (Oasis)
EGYPT
R. Euphrates
ARABIA
ALEXANDER'S CAMPAIGN
ROUTE OF ALEXANDER
ROUTES TAKEN BY HIS GENERALS